D0560560

# Meet the Bitty Twins

Written by Jennifer Hirsch
Illustrated by Stephanie Roth

We're twins—
that means instead of one,
there're two of us,
for twice the fun.

When we wake up, we always say,
"Hello! Hello!" to start our day.

It's easier to make a bed
with two of us to pull the spread.

At breakfast time we like to find
new ways to eat! And we don't mind

if food gets on our pants or dress—
we help each other clean the mess.

It's true, with everything in twos,
we sometimes don't know whose is whose.

Hey, look at this—I found three shoes!

Whose socks are these?
Is this your hat?

It could be mine . . .

No, I'm sure that
belongs to me, but you can borrow
it for now, until tomorrow.

What makes being twins so great?
You always have a fun playmate!

We keep each other company
when making forts or serving tea.

Two can build a bigger castle,

and cleanup's only half the hassle.

Of course, by doing things in double,

we can get in twice the trouble.

One time when we tried to build
a rocket, Mom was not too thrilled.

And when we baked
a giant mud-cake,

it gave Dad a giant headache.

So we tried to make amends

We're not just twins—we're best of friends,

and we think it's a real plus
that there are always two of us!

# *Dear Parents . . .*

Teaching young children to clean up after themselves and help around the house is easier than you might expect! Preschoolers don't view housework as a burdensome chore; to them it's a fun activity that makes them feel important and connected to the adult world.

# Small Jobs for Small Fry

When giving your little one a job to do, keep it simple, and don't expect perfection—the important thing is to get the job done "well enough" with her joyful participation.

Most preschoolers can do these jobs with minimal assistance:

- Put away clean silverware in the drawer
- Pick up and put away toys and books
- Wipe off the table and countertops
- Make the bed

These tasks take some supervision but can still be performed by young helpers:

- Set the table
- Dust with socks on the hands
- Feed pets
- Wipe up a spill

## Kitchen Help

Children especially enjoy helping prepare meals. Let them lend a hand with these kid-friendly kitchen chores:

- Wash and tear up lettuce for green salad
- Pull grapes off stems for fruit salad
- Pour ingredients from the measuring cup into the bowl
- Stir batter or knead dough
- Sprinkle cheese and other toppings on pizza or a casserole

## Don't Overlook the Floor

Kids love to operate gadgets like carpet sweepers, sponge mops, and even small vacuums. You can find mini brush-and-dustpan sets in bright colors—get her one for her very own, and send her to catch the dust mice!

# How to Make a Big Job Fun

- Put on some energetic music. Try to pick everything up before the song (or CD) ends!

- Wave a magic wand and tell your child she's an elephant picking up toys with her trunk or an airplane flying the books back to the shelf.

- Sing this to the tune of "The Farmer in the Dell":
  *It's time to pick up toys, it's time to pick up toys.*
  *We had good fun, and now we're done.*
  *It's time to pick up toys!*
  Make up other lyrics to go
  with the job you're doing.

- If the room is really messy, divide
  the tasks and offer a choice: "Do you want
  to pick up the farm animals, the blocks, or
  the dolls?" Then let her assign you a task!

## Be Generous with Praise

Applaud effort as well as results: "I like how carefully you put away the books" or "You picked up those animals so fast—that's terrific!" Keep your expectations realistic and the experience upbeat, and soon she'll be helping out without even being asked.